Praying for a Miracle
Impossible Things Made Possible

Praying for a Miracle
Impossible Things Made Possible

don wilton

WinePressPublishing
Great Books, Defined.

ISBN 13: 978-1-4141-2229-8
ISBN 10: 1-4141-2229-2
Library of Congress Catalog Card Number: 2011919272

Contents

· ·

Praying for a Miracle

Don Wilton

John 2:1–11

THIS BOOKLET IS about miracles. I am writing about these things because so many of us need a miracle, or two, in our lives. Most of us need many of them because life presents one challenge after another. One lady told me she would need a miracle to take place in order for her marriage to stay intact. Another young mother was told she could never have children of her own. And yet another had sent out over 700 resumes in an effort to find work and believed only a miracle would allow him to provide adequately for the needs of his family.

Miracles happen! I believe this. I do not believe the age of miracles has passed by for the simple reason that God is still very present in our world and very actively engaged in the affairs of people like you and me. Because of Him, miracles have happened, do happen, and will continue to happen. But they may not be what we have made them out to be. In fact much of the truth about miracles has become distorted and the very substance of these wonderful demonstrations of the power of God have become lost in mountainous seas of preacher talk and wishful thinking. As the years have rolled on by, the church, preachers and priests, lonely people, sick people and desperate housewives have all called for or claimed various brands of miracles. Everything from abuse to neglect, fringe theology and fund-raising pretenders have clamored to claim a corner on something that can only belong to the heart of God. Certainly, by definition, some can claim an inevitable miracle that caused them to be in the right place at the right time, but in order for something truly miraculous to take place, God has to be involved all the way.

So, the simple question is, "What is a miracle?" What does the Bible have to say about this? Surely God's Word is the only place we can search to find the truth because it is truth. All of the Bible is true in every way. It is absolute truth. It has no mixture of error. It is not some ordinary book written with the purpose of offering a few insights and suggestions to people. What God says in His book comes from God alone. So, let's go to God's Word and discover what He has to say and to teach us about miracles.

Your life is very important to the Lord Jesus Christ. He wants the best for you and will always work His will in you. So, before despair sets in let us consider some important facts related to miracles.

We begin with three facts about miracles. First, miracles are something only God can do. Otherwise it is not a miracle. Good decisions are possible to make just as the correct medicines can be given to fix a wide assortment of physical problems. There are many times you and I do not feel well, for example, and we end up going to the pharmacy to pick up our doctor's prescription. The medicine works and we are healed. This is wonderful but this is not necessarily a miracle. God has given us common sense and very good doctors to take care of us. And He can work miracles through our doctors—so let's not get ahead of this first fact about miracles. If you can do it or cause it or bring it on, then God has answered your prayers. Perhaps He has used that doctor or that friend—or simply your plain common sense. So, it went well and you passed the test and made it through, for which all of us can rejoice—but what happened was just good sense, clear thinking, self-discipline or something falling in line at the right time and in the right place.

A miracle is something much more. It is miraculous! Let me use two illustrations.

The first is an example of the real blessings of God and, certainly, answered prayer. When I developed a blood clot in my shoulder several years ago, the Lord answered the prayers of many people who love me and interceded for me. He used my doctors to eliminate the problem and He gave me enough sense to embark on courses of action to make certain this does not happen again. As I look back I give all praise and glory to the Lord because He answered our prayers. He blessed me. He worked through those who were qualified to diagnose and eliminate my health problem. In fact, I really believe only the Lord really knows if my situation could be classified as a miracle.

I believe this next example falls into the category of a miracle. When United States Marine 2nd Lt.

Andrew Kinard stepped on that monster in Iraq the blast threw him more than thirty feet up into the air. Both his legs were blown off and he suffered catastrophic injuries in every way. Together with his precious family, a large group of us gathered in the family home and cried out to God. We knew very little and had almost no information. Shortly after Andrew arrived at Bethesda I was privileged to be the first person to walk into his room, while his father, a highly skilled surgeon himself, waited anxiously outside his son's hospital room. What I saw tore my heart out. Let alone the massive injuries, Andrew was hardly recognizable as the vibrant and strapping young man I knew him to be. God gripped my heart intensely. I clearly remember crying out to the Lord—"Oh God, please do something! This is Andrew, Lord! I love him like a son. Besides he is Harry's son, Lord. If for no other reason Lord, do it for Harry and Mary! Lord, Andrew was serving our country. This whole family is faithful to you. Don't let him die Father! He's one of my son Greg's best friends. He has an incredible future. Father, please intervene and do something only You can do. Lord do a miracle in Andrew's life!!" I really do not remember everything I said to God that day, but I was joining with hundreds of people in crying out to the only one who could do something for Andrew. And He did.

As Harry entered the room and saw his son for the first time I knew God was in there with us. From within the unspeakable silence of a stunned father's heart and soul came the powerful presence of the only One who is capable of doing for us what we cannot do for ourselves.

By definition a miracle is a supernatural act requiring supernatural intervention. As Christians we believe only God can do for us what we cannot do for ourselves. If God HAS to be involved in order for it to take place—it can only be a miracle.

Second, miracles are impossible things made possible—only by the Lord Jesus, of course. Again, analysis of the event or happening should produce conclusive evidence that without God's intervention, what happened could not possibly have happened because it was impossible that it did happen! So, take any circumstance in life and ask this question, "Is what I need impossible to accomplish? Can anything human make this happen?" We will see this clearly in the miracle of Jesus when He changed the water into wine. Could a tablet, or a prescription, or a genius, change water into wine? So, miracles can only be defined by possible impossibilities.

Third, miracles are the "show and tell" of God's glory. In a sense they display God for the world to see. They are "bill boards" that contain "pictures" of the power of God to the point at which people are left in wonder and amazement at His goodness and loving care. It is through the means of miracles that our Savior demonstrates His ever-present compassion for His children and His abiding presence. They are designed by God for the benefit of His elect to show a lost and dying world that He alone is God. Miracles demean the notion that God has any rival and establish the fact that He does not share His platform of sovereignty with any other gods.

I have no doubt in my mind that there are many of us who are in desperate need of a miracle right at this moment. We are living in a rather precarious day and age, because the word "miracle" has become abused. Preachers have to exercise great wisdom when referring to others on television, but one only needs to turn on a television set, and it doesn't take long to find a "preacher" who is talking about miracles. You hear statements like, "Send your money, and receive this prayer cloth. If you will only pray with it, you will receive a miracle!" It's a catch-word in today's day and age. "Pay for it, pray with it—and see what God will do for you!" Sounds awful, doesn't it? But sadly true. Many of us have received e-mails instructing us to "Send this e-mail to 10 people and you will receive a miracle." This is not what I'm referring to in this booklet! Miracles come from God at His choosing, but often as the result of a deep and abiding relationship with Him!

Let's think about the wonder of miracles and all the Lord has in store for those who love Him. Others may not know what is going on in your life at this point, but certainly our Savior knows, and He wants you to be fulfilled in every way. You may need the miracle of healing in your body, healing of a relationship, or healing of your heart. You may need a miracle to pay your house payment for the next month. You may need a miracle to find a job in this economy. You may need a miracle to save your marriage, or you may need a miracle to overcome an addiction. Perhaps the son or daughter you love has broken your heart and you are praying for a miracle for your prodigal child to return home.

The Bible teaches us some rather extraordinary things about the issue of miracles. Personally I have become intrigued by the subject to the point that my faith and trust in God has been deepened. I have always known that our Savior does extraordinary things for those He loves, but, after studying the subject of miracles in the Bible, I now find myself praying for others with a far greater sense of expectation in my heart. God does perform miracles today. He will do so for you. I meet people on a daily basis who are constantly searching for miracles. I know a couple whose marriage is falling apart. A wife came to me just recently and said, "Pastor, only a miracle can bring my husband back home again." I've met many parents who have expressed the agony of their hearts concerning their sons and daughters. I would not be surprised if your heart is breaking because of a son, a daughter, or a grandchild, who is not living for the Lord. Maybe you know exactly when they made a decision for Christ, or possibly you wonder if in fact they really did, and you're asking God for a miracle. Not only do individuals or families need miracles, but there are many churches in dire need of a miracle as well. I know people who are praying for miracles in every kind of circumstance of life.

We will examine this subject together, and I believe that God's Word will make application by

His Spirit in your heart and life. I really believe that the Lord Jesus will do for you what you cannot do for yourself. I am praying for every person that reads this booklet! I pray that our Heavenly Father will reach down and touch your heart. I believe that's what God does when you ask Him!

> *"Our Father, we stand amazed in your presence, and we thank you for the inestimable privilege of knowing you as our Savior and Lord. Father, for just a moment, we would consider your Word, for we understand that your Word is a lamp unto our feet and a light unto our pathway. But Father, we are faced by this thing called life. We are praying, Father, for a miracle in our hearts! Lord, we are asking you to reach down from the portals of Heaven and speak to each and every heart within the context of their own circumstances. Father, we are always amazed, because your Word never returns void. Father, we bless your most hallowed name, and we consecrate our lives to you. Speak to us now as we study your Word. We pray these things together in that wonderful name, which is above every name, the name of our Lord and Savior Jesus Christ. Amen."*

The First Miracle

I HAVE HOSTED many wonderful groups of people on trips to Israel for tours of the Holy Land. We visit many different places, but one of the most memorable places is in Cana of Galilee at an historic church called "The Wedding Sanctuary." There I am privileged to officiate at the renewal of the wedding vows of many of the couples in our groups. It is a meaningful experience for those who are involved, but unlike the weddings of Jesus' day, the ceremony only lasts for a short time and each couple is given a certificate commemorating the renewal of their vows before we move on to the next site.

In John chapter two we read the intriguing account of the first miracle Jesus performed in the same area in Cana of Galilee. History books suggest it was traditional during the time of the Lord Jesus Christ to have wedding celebrations that lasted longer than many of our Saturday afternoon weddings of today. They were extraordinary occasions. These happy gatherings were the social functions of the year, and everybody who was anybody received an invitation. In this case, Jesus was among the guests invited. The master of the ceremony usually served the best wine first. This was, most likely, according to the custom of the day. The limited numbers of vineyards in these regions usually meant it was better to serve the best wine when they all arrived at the wedding. The texture of the wine would have been at its fullest, richest and best. Perhaps it was also safest for the host to do this. We all understand the importance of first impressions. Besides, no father of the bride would want to embarrass his daughter at this show-and-tell moment of her life!

As time passed by supplies would begin to dwindle. In anticipation of the pending problem servants would be dispatched to wells with big water pots. Unlike some of the surrounding areas, Galilee was known for its fresh water—even though they didn't drink a lot of it, because it was unsanitary in many instances. What followed is awful but certainly makes much sense. One can perhaps picture the scene as the servants began to add more and more water to the wine they served. Perhaps many of the guests had consumed enough of the "good stuff" to make them a little "tipsy," thereby preventing them from fully appreciating what was being done to them. I am not a connoisseur of wine—never have been, but I am certain that watered down wine was an insult to the host and to the hostess. This did not reflect very well on their social standing. They weren't as concerned about having their nails done properly or wearing the right dress as many are today. Really, the hallmark of a marvelous wedding was the quality of the wine that was served at the table. And, so it was, they would eventually get to the point at which the guests were literally drinking nothing but colored water.

The scene was set. It was time for dramatic action. There was nothing more the father of the bride could do to avert a catastrophe! Then something dramatic happened.

> On the third day a wedding took place at Cana in Galilee. Jesus' mother was there, and Jesus and His disciples had also been invited to the wedding. When the wine was gone, Jesus' mother said to Him, "They have no more wine." "Dear woman, why do you involve me?" Jesus replied. "My time has not yet come."

Although it may appear that Jesus was being rude to His mother this is not an arrogant statement. Jesus was not disrespecting his mother. He was not behaving in a macho way, or being ungentlemanly. Jesus knew that she knew He was capable of fixing this problem. Of all the people who would understand Mary would do so. She had pondered many things in her heart concerning this son she had brought into this world. She knew that this human predicament would present little problem to the Son of man. Perhaps we could put it like this:

"What concern of this is yours? You know better than that mom! You know that my hour has not yet come. You understand that the purpose for which I am in this place has nothing to do with this moment in time, but rather with the sacrifice I am willing to make, because I, the Son of Man, was willing to lay down and lay aside the privilege of being with God in

Heaven, and to take up the mantle of the sinfulness of man, even though I am without sin."

It should come as no surprise, then, that Jesus' mother readily instructed the servants to do whatever it was Jesus would tell them to do. Mary understood one of the most basic of all Christian principles. Just do whatever Jesus tells you to do.

By the way, Jesus had not said anything yet. She just knew. And so, we have this rather remarkable explanation.

> Nearby stood six stone water jars, the kind used by the Jews for ceremonial washing, each holding from twenty to thirty gallons. Jesus said to His servants, "Fill the jars with water"; so they filled them to the brim. Then He told them, "Now draw some out and take it to the master of the banquet."

Why draw them out? Because they couldn't walk around with thirty gallon pots of water, so they had smaller chalices to transport the water. They would literally dip these in and take them, and they would pour that water into the jars that had previously contained the wine. Now, watch what happens here in verse nine:

"When the Chief Servant tasted the water after it had become wine, he did not know where it came from, though the servants had drawn the water he knew. He called the groom and told him, 'Everybody sets out the fine wine first, then after the people have drunk freely, the inferior wine; but you have kept the fine wine until now.' Jesus performed this first sign in Cana of Galilee, and by so doing, displayed His glory, and His disciples believed in Him."

As you pray for your miracle consider this wonderful story. I am sure there are several other reasons why this took place but I want to focus briefly on the top four:

1. **To demonstrate God's power.** The first reason Jesus' miracles are given in the New Testament is as a public demonstration of the ability of God to do what only He can do. What power! If you take that element out of a miracle, you have every reason to question whether or not it is of God. A miracle is something that only God can do!

2. **To glorify God's name.** The second reason miracles happened in the New Testament was

to give glory to the name of God. This passage is pretty evident. One minute the wine was gone, the next they obeyed Him and the water became the finest wine they had ever tasted. Jesus displayed His glory and His disciples believed in Him.

3. **To illustrate man's dependence.** In the words of the hymn writer; "Without Him I can do nothing." Who is man and who am I? Miracles are designed to illustrate man's dependence on God. They had no more wine; there was nothing they could do! Jesus' mother knew they could depend on Him. Perhaps it was from personal experience, or perhaps she had pondered these things in her heart; but nevertheless she knew that only Jesus could solve this problem.

4. **To strengthen man's faith.** As parents we want to teach our children that they can trust us to take care of them. We do that by being faithful to meet their needs physically and emotionally. Every time we feed them, hold them, take care of them when they are sick, and listen to them when they need to talk, we are building trust. It is the same

with our heavenly Father. Every time God does something for me, I trust Him more. When He performs a miracle in my life, He strengthens my faith in Him. Every miracle recorded in the Bible resulted in a stronger faith on the part of those who witnessed it. God is faithful; therefore we can have faith in Him! The first miracle Jesus performed at the wedding in Cana strengthened His disciples' faith in Him.

Just like you, I love this wonderful narrative about Jesus' first miracle. It is no accident because everything Jesus did in His life and ministry was designed for the people He loves. Nothing happened to Him, through Him, or by Him that does not apply to you and me. This wedding was least of all about a wedding and most of all about an incredible miracle. Incredible, yes, unbelievable no! Miracles are incredible things. They are hard to imagine but simple to believe. The simplicity with which we believe in them is the simplicity with which all believers are called on to "walk by faith and not by sight." Faith means we simply trust in God's ability to do all He has promised to do for those who love Him. If you have given your life to Christ by faith it means you have placed your life in His hands and have trusted Him to do above and beyond all you could ask or even think. The miracle you may be looking for is not simply yours for the asking. God is not a simple text message away, even though we can "text" Him at any time with anything we need to tell Him about. Miracles are not just waiting in God's post office for you and me to come by and pick up at our own choosing. No, I believe what took place at Cana provides some key insights into all that the Lord can and will do for us according to His divine will and purpose.

Some of our questions can be answered by taking a closer look at the seven elements present in the miracle that Jesus performed at Cana of Galilee. These seven elements were not only present on this occasion, but they are functional elements of miracles to this day. God hasn't changed His mind. I am completely convinced today as I pray for people who are asking God for a miracle, that a miracle is something that only God can do. This thought is worth repeating over and over again! In my own ministry I am trying to remember this fact.

I love the privilege of being the pastor of a local congregation of people. Like most churches, we have numerous meetings to make decisions regarding the work of the church. Of course there are so many wonderful opportunities to serve the Lord and we do our best to recognize these opportunities. Many of them simply mean we need to "go to work" doing exactly what the Lord has put in our hearts. But we try to remind one another that the greatest work done for Christ is the work we are called to do that we cannot do but for the Lord. Surely the work of the Lord ought to be about doing the things that only God can do. Perhaps we have not raised the bar high enough?

A miracle is something that only God can do, and when He does it. WHEW! We see His glory! I think it's time that we start understanding the actions and the activities of a God who loves us despite ourselves. In our churches, out on the mission field, wherever we are, it seems to me, more and more in our day and age with emerging technology and gadgets, we've come to believe that as long as we're able to do what we think we can do, that God's engaged in what we're doing. Not according to the Word of God! It is time that we fall upon our faces and say, "Oh God, I don't know what else to do." And God says, "Okay, I'll give you a miracle."

I cannot emphasize to you enough that miracles are impossible things made possible by the power of God. Miracles are the show and tell of the power of God. Many of our churches today have forgotten what it means to ask God to do something for us that we cannot do for ourselves.

Most Sunday mornings our ministry team gathers for prayer long before most of our people start arriving for worship. Simply stated our collective prayer is, "Lord, we have prepared a message from God's Word, the choir has practiced for hours on end and the orchestra is ready. Lord, we have an order of worship, and we've done everything we know we ought to do. We are doing it to the best of our ability, but take it all Lord. It all belongs to You and You alone. What we want is a miracle to come down upon this place." And so it ought to be in our personal lives. Perhaps the Lord wants us to do all He tells us to do and then trust Him to do only what He can do. Such is the character of a true miracle.

It would seem to me that there are seven elements present in every miracle. They are presence, predicament, purpose, parameter, practice, power and possibility.

The Seven Elements

1. **Presence**. The Bible says Jesus was there in Cana at the wedding. This miracle would not have taken place without His presence. You take the Lord Jesus Christ out of the equation and you will have no miracle. Do you have Jesus living in you? Have you asked Jesus to come into your heart? Is Jesus with you? You must be sure of this, and you can be sure of this! Salvation is the greatest of all miracles. The fact that a Holy God would forgive your sins against Him and come to live in your heart and life is too amazing. Let alone living eternally with Him in Heaven! Now that's a miracle my friend! Perhaps you need to trust Him as your Lord and Savior right now. Pray this prayer from your heart: "Lord Jesus, I am a sinner. I repent of my sin. Please forgive me of my sins, and come into my heart. I trust in You by faith and receive You into my heart and life." Now remember that His presence is the essential element of any miracle. So, as you look for this miracle, talk to Him, ask

of Him, trust in Him and bless Him when He grants you what you ask for.

2. **Predicament.** The second element of a miracle is predicament. In reality this wedding predicament presented an insurmountable obstacle. The facts were on the table and there was no solution likely. Short of the Master of the ceremony simply calling all the guests together and breaking the bad news to them, nothing could be done to provide them with replenished drinks that tasted good. Their predicament was absolute. They had nowhere to go, nothing to give and no one to turn to. This is why salvation is the greatest miracle! Because Jesus Christ is the only One we can turn to. There is no other way. There are no others who can save us from our sin. The miracle of salvation delivers man from an absolute predicament by which he can never find peace with God except through the Lord Jesus Christ. In the same way, only Jesus' presence can provide the miracle you are praying for when you and I understand that only He can do it. Are you in such a predicament?

3. **Purpose**. The third element of a miracle is purpose. In verse four Jesus explained His purpose. This verse explains the deep things of God and the fundamental purpose for which Jesus Christ died, and why He wants us to be whole again.

4. **Parameter**. The fourth element of a miracle is parameter. Parameters are rules of engagement. Jesus' mother said, "Do whatever He tells you." These were the parameters—just do whatever He tells you. The call of God in my own life began with a clear set of parameters. Well over three decades ago my wife and I were in South Africa where we were born and raised. We were young and had just gotten married. God spoke to us and said, "Go to America." We had no money to even buy a ticket to get here. To complicate things even more, we owed the government money for school loans. There was no way the government would give us permission to move to America. We were in a predicament. We needed a miracle. My wife came to me and said, "We need to sell all of our belongings, wedding gifts included, so we can be obedient

to God." We sold everything we owned, had exactly enough to pay all of our loans to the government of South Africa, buy two tickets to America, with $1400 left in our pocket. Little did we know when we arrived in New York City that $1400 would hardly buy two Big Macs! But we survived. Little did we know that God would use us to teach for many years at the New Orleans Seminary, or that He would use us in such a wonderful ministry to the people at First Baptist Church, in Spartanburg, South Carolina. Little did we know that one day I would be the pastor to Dr. Billy Graham. Little did we know that God would allow me to write books and "share God's truth with a desperate world" through The Encouraging Word broadcast ministry. But God did! He set the rules for engagement and we did our level best to follow them in every way. Another example may involve the challenges many of our young people face today. While I am so grateful for the scores of parents who are really doing such a wonderful job setting parameters for their children and raising them so well, there are some who are "falling through the cracks" of our modern society. This has always been true in every generation. But the world is changing at such a rapid rate. And with this change has come an avalanche of new challenges for our kids. In today's world it is really hard to set parameters, let alone to know what parameters to set! We must pray for our teenagers! So, if you are praying for a miracle in the life of one of your children, just think about the fact that Jesus set an entire pattern for the servants to follow—in order for them to receive their miracle.

5. **Practice.** The fifth element of a miracle is practice. The servants went out and did exactly what Jesus told them to do. Are we willing to be obedient and do exactly what Jesus tells us to do? Once we know the parameters, are we willing to follow whatever he tells us? I was playing with my grandson, Bolt, recently and we had toys scattered all over the place. When it was time to clean up, I said, "Bolt, it's time to put all the toys away. Big Chief (that's my grandfather name) has to go and get on an airplane now." Bolt

picked up one toy, threw it into the toy box and said, "Did it!" I must admit it was really cute, but I had to explain to little Bolt that all the toys had to be put in the toy box. How many times does God give us the parameters and we do one thing He tells us to do, but we do not finish the job? We must do exactly what Jesus tells us to do.

6. **Power.** The sixth element of a miracle is power. In Verse 10, the power of God was demonstrated, and God in His infinite wisdom, and by His mighty power, through his Son, the Lord Jesus Christ, demonstrated that the best indeed can be served last. God's power cannot always be easily seen or defined. When Harry Kinard stepped into the room with Andrew for the first time God's power was there. As Christians we just know it. We feel it. The Holy Spirit reveals it! Perhaps we are not looking for His power? Perhaps we are not trusting in His power? God's power is the manifestation of Himself in ways we cannot necessarily describe. It is the demonstrated action of God who does what He does just because He is God! Often

we see God's power in the rear view mirror. And often we are privileged to bear witness to his power right then and there! On the spot, so to speak. Ask the Lord to open your spiritual eyes so that you can see his power. And, when you do see His power, thank Him first, and then tell everyone you possibly can tell. Bear witness to the power of God. In so doing, you may be bearing witness to an extraordinary act of God—a miracle!

7. **Possibilities**. The seventh element of a miracle pertains to the limitless potential and endless possibilities that God brings to bear on all who love Him. Herein lies the contagious effect of miracles. What the Lord does for you He intends to be used to glorify His name everywhere. This is what we read about in verse eleven of this great story—all the people were blessed. It's the contagious effect of a miracle of God. When God moves, the possibilities are endless. I know a lady who has spent the better part of her life living in sin. Sadly, she still just doesn't get it. She has repeatedly turned her back on the Lord. Her parents have almost given up. She's now

close to 50 years of age and has gone through many "ups and downs." She carries tremedous hurt and pain in her heart, some with great cause. She has been treated unjustly, has been abused, has been neglected—and she has brought much on herself too. This lady has made many poor choices in life, has been rebellious and disobedient, has defied and decried authority and has walked away from many gestures of love and grace. Above all else, she has refused to surrender to the Lordship of Christ who demands our everything. Oh yes indeed. This lady is incredibly gifted. She has much to offer the Lord. She has such a vibrant personality. But the years are going by and she simply will not surrender her life to the Lordship of Christ. We are praying now for a miracle. Only God can do what only God can do. We believe it! And, what's more—we believe that when He does—well, the best is yet to be!

$\cdots\cdots\cdots\cdots\cdots\cdots\cdots\cdots\cdots\cdots\cdots\cdots$

Seven Steps to a Miracle

I DON'T KNOW what kind of problems you may
be dealing with, but I do know that the Lord has
impressed on me some practical steps to take in
this regard. To make them a little easier to follow
I have labeled them "The Seven Steps in Praying
for a Miracle". I know you will "tweak" them to
suit your own need for a miracle without stepping
outside of what God's Word teaches. I am trying to
practice these steps in my life and I know what a
tremendous blessing they have been to hundreds
of other people as well. Ask God to speak to you as
you read these steps. Get a sheet of paper and write
them down. Put them in your Bible. Tape them on

your mirror. Keep them in your car as you travel. Keep them before you as you pray for those things in your life. These are practical steps. You can use them in your church, your personal life, and to help other people. They include, identify what is going on, write it down, form partnerships, pray, follow instructions, anticipate, and respond.

The Seven Steps

1. **Identify what is going on.** The greatest problem most people have is that they refuse to identify the problem they're having. It is easy to sweep a problem under the carpet and pretend it does not exist. On the other hand, it is easy to think the problem is one thing, when it is really something all together different. Be honest with yourself and ask God to help you identify the real issue.

2. **Write it down.** Every time I meet with my staff and with our ministry team, I continually tell them to write down their idea or plan. If you can't write it, you don't know it. You know there are just thousands of people who have wonderful ideas, but until you write it down, it'll always just be an idea.

3. **Form partnerships**. Form partnerships with other Christians—purpose-driven partnerships! All of us know precious people who are God anointed, grace filled people who are prayer warriors and partners in the ministry to which we've been called. Go to those people. This is not a matter of just selecting someone. Pray about it and form a partnership with the person God lays on your heart. Perhaps this may be a Bible-study group you enjoy, or a prayer group. Share your issue with them and ask them to pray with you about it in a meaningful way. Open your heart to them and, if needed, ask them to keep your situation confidential. In fact, if your need for a miracle is very personal, then I would counsel you to only choose one person perhaps. It still amazes me how many confidential things are passed around churches in the name of "prayer requests."

4. **Pray**. Just do it. Often we talk about our prayer requests to our friends until we are blue in the face, and we never get around to talking to God! I've been married for over 30 years to the most beautiful girl in the

world. When I first met Karyn, I remember dating her, and that was the first time I really began to learn about prayer. In our very early dating months I even recall a rather humorous incident involving prayer. When the time came for me to drop my "girl" off at her dorm after one of our dates I felt the "urge" to kiss her like she had never been kissed before! All the other couples around us were! At the very moment of impact Karyn stopped me and said, "Why don't we have a word of prayer together?" I was shocked and devastated to the core!! I can hear you laughing but she really did this to me. I think I had just learned my first real lesson about prayer! Seriously, that was the beginning of God doing something incredible in my life. He did and continues to work miracles in my life to this day. We often talk about prayer, but I submit to you there is nothing more significant than getting down to business and having a conversation with our Heavenly Father. Pray! Just do it! Your Heavenly Father wants an intimate relationship with you. You can say things to God that you cannot say to anyone else. Matthew 6:6–15 gives us instructions on how to pray. Take a moment now to read these verses. Jesus tells us to go into our prayer closet, or private place, close the door, and have an intimate conversation with Him. You do not need to be concerned about what you say. Your Father knows what you need before you say it, but He does want you to ask. If you continue to read these verses you will see that Jesus talks about forgiveness. Jesus reiterates the idea of prayer and forgiveness in other places in the Bible as well. In Mark 11:25, Jesus says, "When you stand praying, if you hold anything against anyone, forgive him, so that your Father in heaven may forgive you your sins." Sin hinders our relationship with God. In order to pray for a miracle, we must have our lives in order with others and with God.

I received a phone call late one night from Dr. Billy Graham. He was at the Mayo Clinic and called to ask a question. Now folks, I do not believe he wanted an answer from me, I believe he wanted me to think. I have never been around a more humble or precious man. He talks to me about deep spiritual issues. His question to me was this, "Why did Paul pray and supplicate?" After much discussion we came to the conclusion that prayer is talking to God, but supplication is the attitude with which we speak to God. We must ask God for a miracle in an attitude in which we find ourselves coming into the presence of the King of kings and the Lord of lords. We have been given permission through the righteousness of God in Jesus Christ to come into holy presence. When I pray I am not calling the White House to ask a favor from the President of the United States. I'm not calling my local city councilman. I'm not merely going to my pastor. I am coming into the presence of Almighty God who is the Creator of the universe! God can do exceedingly abundantly above all that you and I ask or even think! Do you really believe that?

5. **Follow instructions.** Your prayer conversation with the Savior is a two way street. You talk to God, and He talks back to you. In the Lord's Prayer, Jesus said, "Thy will be done

on earth as it is in Heaven," but evidently as we try to understand what it means to have Heaven on earth, there are many of us who get on our faces and we ask God to do what only God can do, and when He tells us what to do, we don't do it. The truth is there are so many of us who just simply will not listen to God's instructions—let alone follow His instructions. I really believe that disobedience has become the scourge of the local New Testament church. This is a great struggle and challenge in my own life. I don't know how many times I have asked God to do something in my life—to do what only God can do, and I've been willing to identify it, to write it down, and to even form partnerships with gracious, godly men and women, and to seek God's face in prayer, but I have flat out refused to follow God's instructions. If your marriage is in trouble and you begin to go through the steps to receive a miracle, you will hear instructions from God that will be difficult to follow through on such as: "Take your wife on a date. Say you are sorry. Admit that you were wrong. Ask for forgiveness. Change your habits. Cut off ungodly relationships with the opposite sex. Get home on time." You will receive many instructions from God. But the question is, "Are you willing to follow instructions?" We must be obedient to God's instructions before we can witness His miracles!

6. **Anticipate.** What a great word! Many times in my life, I have asked God for something and then I am surprised when He gives it to me! You want God to do something in your life that only God can do? Anticipate! The great Methodist preacher, John Wesley coined that phrase that we've grown to love so much—"Attempt great things for God; expect great things from God." Somehow in our theological context, we've become so pharisaical, and we've become so insipid within our own little cocoons, in our own religiosity, and deep sense of spirituality, that we have lost what it means to anticipate and expect an outpouring from a God who loves us despite ourselves. Many preachers have lost that great expectation of believing that God's word will never return void, and when

we stand in God's pulpit Sunday by Sunday, we've lost that keen sense of anticipation that God is in the saving business, and that Jesus Christ died for us. Probably the best example of anticipation was Jesus' mother. She didn't know what Jesus was going to do, or how he was going to do it, but she believed that He would do it. The word, "anticipate," points to a rejuvenation of the heart and gives believers framework in which to formulate an expectancy that God is actually the God of miracles. The expectancy that God can do the impossible.

7. **Respond.** This final step is so important. At the very heart of the issue is gratitude. Remember the seven lepers Jesus told us about? God did a miracle in their lives and only one of them bothered to come back and say thank you. When God does a miracle in your life, how do you respond? Where's the testimony? A living testimony is still a vital component of God's means to connect with the people He loves. Have you noticed that there seems to be less and less of a demand and a mandate for people to stand up and

say "Jesus Christ has changed my life?" There's nothing more wonderful than the testimony of a changed life. If you are praying for a miracle I would strongly suggest you pre-determine the fact of your testimony. Make a commitment in heart and prayer that you will make known the wonderful hand of the living God in your life. Perhaps you may even tell your accountability partners of your intent and purpose to testify. It would be good for them to remind you of your promise. And, just try and imagine the numbers of people who will be greatly blessed by hearing about the way in which you prayed for a miracle—and God did it!

The Greatest Miracle

E'VE TALKED ABOUT miracles all through this booklet, but actually I have saved the best until last. We often need a miracle or simply want a miracle. Everyone wants to be a part of something bigger than themselves. We often go through life and miss the greatest miracle of all. A miracle is something that only God can do! You may need the greatest miracle of all … that is, the miracle of salvation! Only God can forgive our sin! Only God can save a sinner! Only God can redeem a person! Often we pray and pray and pray for a miracle, but if you have never accepted Jesus into your heart and experienced the greatest miracle of all, then all of your other prayers are futile. You can be sure of your salvation today! You can know that you know that you know you are saved and have experienced the greatest miracle of all. Once you accept Jesus into your heart, the Holy Spirit will come into your heart and life. He will guide you, convict you, and show you how to pray for the miracles you need in your life. If you have never accepted Jesus Christ as your Savior I would like to offer you this opportunity to act now. These three steps to experience the greatest miracle ever all come straight out of the Bible.

1. **Admit that you are a sinner.** The Bible teaches, "All have sinned, and come short of the glory of God." (Rom. 3:23) We must realize we are born with a sin nature and there is nothing we can do about it in our own strength.

2. **Believe in your heart that Jesus died on the cross for your sins.** This is a heart issue, not a brain issue. Believing in your heart is the key! Believe that Jesus is the only way to be forgiven of your sins. He is the perfect sacrifice before a holy God! (Eph. 2:8)

3. **Confess with your mouth that you are a sinner and that He is Lord of all.** Believing

in your heart in the first step, but you must confess it with your mouth as well. (Rom. 10:9)

4. **Repent from your sins**. Turn and walk in the opposite direction. When Christ comes into your life, you will be made a new creation. (Acts 3:19)

5. **Surrender your life to God.** When you pray and ask God to forgive you, He will put the Holy Spirit into your heart and life to work through you. When you give up and allow the Holy Spirit to work through you, you can conquer sin in your life. He will take away your sins and put His righteousness in you. (Matt. 16:24)

You can pray a prayer something like this:

Dear God, I know that I am a sinner. I know that I am separated from you by my sin. I know that on my own, I can do nothing to save myself. Only Jesus can save me. I believe in my heart that Jesus died on the cross for my sins. I accept what He did as a payment for my sins. I confess that you are Lord. I ask you to come into my heart and life today to save me. I give my entire life to you today. I surrender my life to you. I ask you to walk with me and guide me in my life. Lord, I ask you to speak to me and help me know how to live my life. I thank you for saving me today! In Jesus' name I pray. Amen

When you take the above steps, then God in His power performs the greatest miracle known to man. You will become as white as snow. Your sins will be forgiven. When God looks at you, He will only see Jesus and what He did on the cross for you. He will change you from the inside out! Then you can begin your new life in Christ. You can begin to pray for miracles in your life according to His will. The Holy Spirit will show you how to pray. You will begin to walk with Him, and He with you. You will know when to pray for a miracle and you will begin to recognize miracles in your life on a daily basis.

I pray that God will touch your heart and life today as you begin to pray for miracles in your life. God is good! He wants to give you miracles! He wants to bless your life. Be mindful to tell others about Him and his goodness as you live your life and experience His miracles!

Sidebar: We would love to hear from you! If God has truly performed a miracle in your life, we want to know. You can contact us by going to www.theencouragingword.org or you can follow me on Twitter @don_wilton